KING OF THE JEWS

Poems

Matthew Lippman

Teaneck, New Jersey

KING OF THE JEWS ©2025 Matthew Lippman. All rights reserved. No part of this book may be used or reproduced in any manner whatsoever without written permission except in the case of brief quotations embodied in critical articles and reviews.

Published by Ben Yehuda Press
122 Ayers Court #1B
Teaneck, NJ 07666

http://www.BenYehudaPress.com

To subscribe to our monthly book club and support independent Jewish publishing, visit https://www.patreon.com/BenYehudaPress

Jewish Poetry Project #60   http://jpoetry.us

Ben Yehuda Press books may be purchased at a discount by synagogues, book clubs, and other institutions buying in bulk. For information, please email markets@BenYehudaPress.com

ISBN13 978-1-963475-79-1 pb

25 26 27 28 / 10 9 8 7 6 5 4 3 2   250825

Advance Praise for Matthew Lippman's *King of the Jews*

How does one respond to the terror of Oct 7? For Matthew Lippman, it's through poetry. In *King of the Jews*, Lippman names many who perished, were kidnapped, held hostage. He names friends, students, rock stars, too. Lippman honors—and loves—them all. He even anoints them king, *King of the Jews*. Whether talking with his dog on the morning six hostages were found murdered or with Chabad boys on the ferry to Ellis Island, Lippman takes us straight to the heat, the "center of the earth ... the center of the name." These poems hold the beauty and the horror of the world and the deep longing, living within Lippman's naked, aching heart. From Brooklyn to Brookline, Jerusalem to the Golan Heights, we all share one joy, one pain: "No matter what you do as a Jew / you grieve as a Jew." Hail, hail, *King of the Jews*. Matthew Lippman, Kol Hakavod.
—**Diane Gottlieb**, editor of *Manna Songs: Stories of Jewish Culture & Heritage*

Matthew Lippman has long been my poet king— for making me feel seen and heard, remembered and alive, for his rock-n-roll hand in laughter and sadness, and for his unique ability to do through poetry "what kings do/they make people see what their best selves can be." Once again, if impossibly, Lippman manages to revive the human spirit with *Kings of the Jews*. Here is a lyrical, post 10/7 Book of Lamentations— a book that did not want to be written, should never have been written, but which pours, dirge-like, from every crack in the grieving poet's heart, spilling out, name by name, story by story, song by doleful song, into the diasporic aftermath of this darkest day in recent memory, urging us amid the continued horror to "to remember that we are all people, and we must not forget."
—**Sara Lippmann**, author of *Leech*.

For Rachel

Contents

Avinu Malkeinu / 1

    CHAI

Breaking of the Vessels / 5
They Are All Kings / 6
Always Eastern Parkway Getting Spiritual / 8
My Daughter Cried this Morning When the Hostages Were Dead / 9
Brooklyn Is Always the Kingdom of the Jews / 10
Hear My Voice Hersh / 11
Nakedness Is the King / 12
The Cobbler / 13
This Is About Staying Alive / 14
King of the Jews King of the Trees / 16
The Quivering King of the Jew / 17
Madness and Sorrow Into Your Ribcage / 19
Homeostasis Is King of the Jews / 20
Shalom My Dears / 21
Bread-Of-Affliction Is King of the Jews / 22
The Only Sound of Feeling Good About Something in the Distance / 23
Sweet Talkin' King Jew / 24
But Inside the Rain / 25

    DOUBLE CHAI

Chai Everlasting / 29
Revelation Pants / 30
Golf Jews / 32
The Köln Concert Is King of the Jews / 33
Not That Kind of Jew / 35
King of the Jews in His Joy / 36
Juan Is the King Sauce of Peace / 37
Like Oranges and Holy Land / 38
Crush the Half Notes So Holy / 39
Shofar Party / 40
Danielle Haim Is King of the Jews / 42

Your Sunflower Field Life / 43
We Bow to the Floor to Pray / 44
Led Zeppelin Is King of the Jews on Kol Nidre / 45
She Was Queen of the County and the King of Love / 46
Form Follows Function Is King / 47
The Sukkah Is King of the Jews / 48
King of the Jews Is One Word / 49
Will You Help with These Sheets Please / 50
Acknowledgements: / 52
About the Author / 53

King of the Jews

Avinu Malkeinu
(almighty and merciful)

When I sat in synagogue,
I did not look at the rabbi.
I watched the trees.
Avinu Malkeinu.
Our father our king.
I couldn't get my eyes off the trees
in their nakedness and green.
Their green moving into yellow
moving into red and death,
their dying leaves and the restoration of the spirit.
What does that mean? To restore a spirit?
It means that humility is a disappearance into a nakedness no one has ever seen.
Avinu Malkeinu.
I sat in synagogue and couldn't keep my eyes off the trees.
I wanted to fall into them barefoot and pregnant with the world and the rabbi
    vanished.
I wanted to take off my Rosh Hashana synagogue clothes
and walk into the trees to be my rabbi,
to be my Torah,
to be my casting off of all the sins.
We have sinned, brother.
We bomb villages.
We hide in corners and eat sugar.
We look away from the homeless people and lock our car doors.
We steal from the bakery.
We blow up oil fields in the name of God
and say bad things about people behind their backs.
Avinu Malkeinu.
I wanted to walk naked into the trees
out of the sanctuary
into the sanctuary of autumn trees
and fall to the ground,
my flesh torn and soft,
my muscles like birds
whistling out of my body—
little missiles crashing through the air in song.

CHAI

Breaking of the Vessels

This morning, I became King of the Jews.
They found 6 dead hostages, and the dog walked me into the center of earth.
I was not King of the Jews but when we got there,
I was most certainly King of the Jews
and I was nowhere and everywhere
and all the hostages were dead, and we were all of the hostages, everywhere,
all of us,
taken by a history with so many words
there is nothing left to say.
Because when you are in a tunnel, and they blow your face off
there is no such thing as the past.
The dog said, *Come on boychick,*
and I said, *Where are we going?*
and she said, *We are already there*
and when we arrived
there we were,
all of us Jews
and the hostages were gone
and they had names
and these are their names,
Hersh and Alexander and Carmel and Eden and Ori and Almog.
And the center of the earth was the center of their names and so I asked the dog,
Why are you taking me there?
and then I wept.
At the center of the earth, I broke open and said to the dog,
Now, I am King of the Jews,
and she said, *Yes you are.*
And she said,
It means you are everywhere and nowhere in the center of the earth,
in the center of the name,
and that's when everything got obliterated and everything became clear
and the dog was finally done doing its business.

They Are All Kings

Natalie and Ben and Ori and Eliora are King of the Jews on Tuesdays and
    Saturdays.
on Sundays and Wednesdays.
They go to their King of Jews Mall
and spend money at Sephora and Shake Shack.
They walk around in their Lululemon shorts and gold chains,
their homes in Roslindale and Newton and Brookline
and hold hands and pretend there is love
because there is love.
They talk about boys and girls and car washes and happiness
and get lonely with each other and far away
their Israeli counterparts are doing the same thing,
but not the same thing.

Natalie and Ben and Ori and Eliora are the suburban King of the Jews in
    an America
that does not like Jews
but they don't care, these teenagers wearing their Jewish stars and chais
trying to fit in, never fitting in,
saying *fuck you everyone*
we are King of the Jews
walking the aisles of CVS
buying hair product and paste-on-nails and bags of flamin' hot Cheetos
while their Israeli counterparts listen to Asaf Avidan and dance
in the wake of sorrow and survival.

They are all kings, Natalie and Ben and Eliora and Ori,
late night Facetiming and laughing and holding steady in their own secret
    sorrow
because what they know is that their Israeli counterparts
are their brothers and sisters no matter the music—
the Taylor Swift, the Noa Kirel the Bal Shem Tov Baruch Hashem
dancing done in the dust and fields of parking lots and desert daylight.

It's a sad world.
It's a beautiful world

and these kings make me feel like I am part of something that has nothing to
 do with me,
like my time has come and gone
and so I will pick them up in my little bent out of shape Toyota
anywhere anytime
when they call and tell me they've run out of money, it's late and they are tired
and can I get them,
they will be in front of the movie theater at Legacy Place,
right next to J.P. Licks
and the falafel street vendor, Moshe,
on some street in Jerusalem that I don't know—
have never been—but don't worry, I will find it,
I will come and get you.

Always Eastern Parkway Getting Spiritual

I was on the ferry to Ellis Island or The Statue of Liberty
and there were these three boys wearing tzitzit
so I sat next to them on the way to Ellis Island
to feel part of something
and we began to talk like we knew we were all Jews.
One kid told me they were from California, Palisades,
and their school burned down during the wildfires,
his name was Jonah or Ezra or David
and that he and his school were in New York for a Chabad retreat,
kids from all over the country,
770 Eastern Parkway, always New York,
always Eastern Parkway getting spiritual
and we talked about learning, fires, forgetting,
and one of them said, *Why do you like New York?*
and it was kippahs everywhere and I didn't have mine
or an answer to his question
but it didn't matter
it never fucking matters to the rest of the world that our grandparents, great-grandparents
and uncles, aunts, cousins, brothers and sisters
were on a long-ago boat together.
Today, we were on the boat together from Ellis Island or away from Ellis Island,
to some dream that is either still alive or has died real quick.
The wind was crazy and the seagulls were nuts
and the world was a barometer with no more mercury in its guts
and when the boat docked we got off to be with our respective school groups
and you know what they said to me? They said,
Be safe.

My Daughter Cried this Morning When the Hostages Were Dead

When my daughter, who transferred to Brandeis says,
I'm glad I don't have to start the year at the other school,
she is the King of the Hebrews.
When she benched on Friday after the Shabbat meal
with strangers she already knew
they were the whole state of Israel, and they were,
altogether, King of the Jews.
After Havdalah she was up late and heard the news.
There is always news.
Why is there always news about the Jews?
My wife said, *Did you hear the news?*
A bunch of students were chased for being Jews
by a whack job with a broken glass bottle.
My daughter cried this morning when the hostages were dead.
They have been dead for 2 days and a million years.
They were dead before there were stars,
right before there were stars,
and the light from 13.8 billion years that has just reached us
is an elegy to their lives.
Jews are astrophysics and astronomy.
Jews are stardust and dust.
So is everyone
who has faith.
My daughter has faith.
She put her face in the illuminated hiss from 13.8 billion years ago
and lit up like she was on a throne for the rest of us
about to sing the flame.

Brooklyn Is Always the Kingdom of the Jews

Marisa is King of the Jews tonight.
I don't even know where Marisa is right now
although I expect she is in Brooklyn which is always the kingdom of the Jews.
That's what Shirley told me on Ocean Avenue when I was 8.
Brooklyn is the Israel of the United States
and then she gave me a plate of sable and told me to fuck off.
Not Marisa.
She never told me to fuck off.
She met Hersh's cousin on the street somewhere in the Golan Heights of
    Canarsie.
No matter what you do as a Jew
you grieve as a Jew,
you grieve as a human being on the planet earth before there was an earth.
I don't care if you are sucking down a Cherry Lime Rickey at Bendix Cafe in
    Chelsea
with Mike 30 years before Oct. 7th.
Fuck Oct. 7th.
That's why Ms. Schwartz runs the lot of us, the Jews.
Because she knows madness and she knows civilization and she knows
how to hold her children in their 20s
when there is too much sorrow even the Staten Island Ferry knows.
She runs us all like a well-greased Mercedes engine block
because she can find a pickle of joy in a smorgasbord of demise.
Really, go to Brooklyn if you don't believe me.
I implore you, go,
and run into her on Court Street near Carroll
where the A and G Pork Store is still in business
and you can get a half a pound of prosciutto
for just under 20 bucks
even if you do keep kosher
but need to get out for just a sec.

Hear My Voice Hersh

Hersh's mother, she knows what's up.
Tonight, her son is dead, and we eat steak.
How can we eat rib eye?
With grilled squash?
I burned my fingers on the grill and my lord, her son is dead.
My wife said, *She went to the border, put up a structure, grabbed a megaphone and screamed, Hersh, I want to talk with you so I am talking with you.*
How might you say that in Hebrew?
Tonight, we ate steak and how do you live 11 months with half an arm.
Hersh's mother grabbed a megaphone and screamed into Gaza,
Hear my voice, Hersh, I am here.
How do you howl that in Hebrew?
She grabbed the megaphone, and it was a staff
and we ate skirt steak marinated in a soy, balsamic, garlic glaze.
I did not scream when I burned my finger on the grill plates.
I did not complain.
Her son is dead.
You always have to think about that for the rest of your days
when you get a mosquito bite
or the 1 train does not stop at 238th street for track repair
or you get a flat tire on I-80 headed into Iowa City.
You cannot moan and cry and complain.
Rachel knew he was dead even before he was dead.
She is King of the Jews today, and tomorrow,
and from now into eternity,
back into eternity.
13.8 billion light years back.
That's what she screamed into the megaphone across the border into Gaza.
Hersh, we are coming for you.
You can't even imagine the silence that followed
even when it was so quiet
all that existed was the dust of stars rolling around
on the tip of her tongue.

Nakedness Is the King

Nakedness is King of the Jews.
That's how I imagined they found their bodies.
Naked.
Even if they had shirts on, blue jeans, torn underwear.
They were naked.
Aren't you tired of nakedness as a Jew?
You go into a Starbucks and everyone undresses you.
Jew.
Head into a Cheesecake Factory, a Publix, Central Park at 72nd Street.
Jew. Jew. Jew.
That's why we are kings.
Because we are always undressed to be seen.
Throw them in the ovens.
Naked.
Pour Lyme on their heads.
Jew.
Shove them against a tunnel wall and pull the trigger. Unclothed.
Stripped down and bare.
Aren't you tired of that kind of nakedness?
It's been the kind of nakedness all of us have had to endure
as long as there has been time.
Oh, look at those Jews.
Those dirty Jews.
I want to be a naked Jew in Times Square
and no one says, *Ugly Jew.*
Poor Jew.
King of them all.
I want to be butt naked in Yellowstone National Park and Yosemite
and running unclothed on the Autobahn to keep up
and there are no eyes.
Let me be a Jew in Auschwitz, 1944, naked and fat, King of the Jews,
and no one cares one bit,
not one person pulls out their cattle car and throws open the door.

The Cobbler

Sandler makes me happy.
He's just a guy in big shorts and long shirts.
He does not care and there is no war in his heart.
When he made the movie *The Cobbler*
there was a seriousness in his cheeks and no war in his heart.
He was king of my people.
The first 4 minutes of *The Cobbler are in Yiddish.*
Who does that?
Who has the chutzpah to do that?
If I had not seen the rest of the movie, I would have still given it The Oscar for Best Picture.
It's a terrible picture.
It's one of those terrible beautiful pictures that makes you cry, especially if you are a Jew. Even if you are not a Jew.
All those shoes.
There are pickles in it and Steve Buscemi plays a Jewish barber and he's Italian.
That's what is so important about humanity.
We are all so close to one another even though the vowels are different.
In *The Cobbler*, Adam's character saves his family with a multitude of shoes.
It's not a Jewish theme
but there are shoes everywhere
and Method Man is in it.
He plays a good guy and a bad guy, sometimes in the same scene.
He makes me happy, too.
At the end of the movie Dustin Hoffman shows up and he's sad, not like he was in *Tootsie*.
Like an endless Jewish sadness into an infinity of joy of Sandler.
He even speaks a little Yiddish,
Mshpokh libe iz di bester libe,
then disappears in baggy shorts and a double-x t-shirt that screams *New York Knicks.*

This Is About Staying Alive

Steve S. is King of the Jews because I saw him at Wegmans
and he was wearing an IDF t-shirt.
It was purple and said something in Hebrew but I was lost.
I have been lost for so many years
so I walked up behind him and said, *You sexy motherfucker,*
and he said, *Hey,* elongating the 'ey' into the Wegman's hot bar
with all the lemon and pepper wings.
His daughter and my daughter used to be best friends
and once he called me up to go see Fleetwood Mac at TD Garden.
That's how bad ass he is
so I said, at the Wegman's self-checkout aisle,
You are King of the Jews, and he said, *No,*
I'm just a representative,
which was when I heard someone call my name,
coming at me from the other end of the store,
where they keep the Half-n-Half and Steve said,
Pay attention,
and he was right
but I couldn't focus
and I heard my name again.
It was still far off, getting more faint,
coming from the other end of the store,
maybe where they keep the kosher chicken and Doritos
and Steve said,
You workin' now?
   because the last time I saw him was at Wegmans
during the summer months
and I told him the story about how I got fired
for not paying attention to the birds
and he said, *Ain't that a pisser,* meaning,
it's always something when you don't pay attention to the wings and feathers.
He said,
We have to get a drink sometime soon,
but I was sad and I said so
and I could still hear the last four letters of my name, *thew,* floating above the
   broccoli

but it was disappearing into the sky and sounded like *thaw*
and I said, *Let me pay for your provisions,*
but this wasn't about money,
this was about staying alive,
and that's when his 6-foot-6 frame bent down to hug me,
more like hold me,
and he said, *Let's not disappear now,*
and that's why Steve S. is King of the Jews
because he won't let you forget,
he will never let any of us forget.

King of the Jews King of the Trees

The morning after 10/7 I went to the pool at the local Young Men's
    Christian Association
to clean out my blood. Or something.
Matty B. was already in the water and mid-stroke he stopped and said:
I am with you brother.
Matty B. is the mayor of West Roxbury.
He owns a landscaping business called *Thoreau Landscaping.*
What's up with that? I asked him once in the steam room.
Trees make magic, he told me.
Matty B. is King of the Jews King of the Trees
I don't care how Irish Catholic he is.
Or something.
This morning, I saw him at Dunkin'.
He screamed my name, *Matty.*
I screamed back, *Matty.*
He was talking to his West Roxbury boys.
It was a TV commercial for the local community station that would never
    be made.
Or something that meant we live in a neighborhood.
Matty B. is the neighborhood.
You need a good neighbor?
Matty is right down the street
even if he's walking the beach with his boys in Barnstable.
He's King of the Jews.
On the morning of 10/8,
he stopped his breaststroke and entered the moment.
It's still happening, the moment,
because it never goes away and
almost a year later Matty B. enters it every time we find each on the block.
This morning, I saw him at Dunkin'
with a large dark roast in his left hand.
He held a staff in his right
or it was a shaft of light from the new day sun or something,
some thing that eviscerates the horror by doing its best
to enter the horror
and then climb its tree.

The Quivering King of the Jew

I had this thing happen to me today while in synagogue.
I don't know Hebrew
and the hostages were murdered, and Israel is burning
and I have never been to Jerusalem
and this thing happened to me in synagogue
when some song was being sung
or when the Torah came out of the ark
or the light slithered through a window.
This quivering happened to me, that was it, yes, a quivering,
when I looked across the room
and a woman smiled at me, a Jew,
all these Jews in all this Shabbat,
it happened to me
and I couldn't take my eyes off of it
because there was nothing to see
when the light slithered through the Torah
and I couldn't handle it, this thing, this thing that happened,
and maybe it was the kind of thing that happened to all those old dudes
in the Old Testament as it was told to them by God,
that I saw God, or no,
that God was closer than God had ever been before
like the moon.
Like the moon at the horizon when its big head radiates red.
Something happened to me and maybe God put its hand on my neck for a second
and I could barely see or breathe or stand.
But I couldn't hang on or I was about to lose my mind
into some pure distinction of a living
that had nothing to do with me
and all those hostages were killed and here was the thought,
Does it take 6 hostages to get you to God?
The chutzpah. The hubris. The horror.
But I had no answer because I wasn't thinking about questions.
I just couldn't stop crying and not because the spirit moved me, it went beyond that,
and I know my friend Terry will know what I mean

even though he's a preacher and I have never met him in my life
but he knows what not being able to hold on is
and it was not grief
and it was not the ecstatic
I just said to myself, *Oh, this is it*,
right there in the sanctuary;
this is why God has no face and no name and no words
and I was not King of the Jews
but I wanted someone to be,
I wanted someone to talk with, to say, *What is this thing happening to me?*
Help.
And maybe it was the 6 dead hostages
or maybe it was just not being able to stand it,
being in this world
in this holy house
on your sabbath
the kingdom doors flung wide open and then what do you do
and what, finally, have you become?

Madness and Sorrow Into Your Ribcage

I can't tell if the morning is beautiful or not so beautiful
but when I stopped at the Sudbury Reservoir to watch the mist rise into
    the red leaves,
I said to the morning, *You are a beautiful morning.*
But that made me sad
because I couldn't tell who was King of the Jews—
Carmel Gat or her cousin Gil Dickmann.
The Hamas bastards took Carmel from Kibbutz Be'eri
where she led yoga and meditation to smooth out the heart;
where 10/7 started out with much sunshine and many oranges
then turned into a day with no light and less citrus.
After months in the darkness
Gil Dickmann and a group of mothers and fathers and uncles and aunts
of the hostages
couldn't stand the reality of captivity anymore
and tried to storm Gaza
to free their loved ones
but the army stopped them, and Carmel Gat was killed,
and Gil Dickmann said,
We could have saved them all.
I am not sure if that is true, but I believe it is true.
Sometimes you have to smash madness and sorrow into your rib cage,
mix them together in the center of your body
so you are a little human grenade of resistance
and you can do anything
because you are a superhero called King of the Jews.
This morning the morning was only the morning;
it was stunning in sweetness
and I imagined I saw Carmel Gat in her Lotus pose
hovering in the mist
rising off of the Sudbury Reservoir as some kind of guardian angel,
I'm sure of it, of this I am sure.

King of the Jews

Homeostasis Is King of the Jews

Mark tells me Eno is an antisemite, and I say, *Oh no,
I thought he was King of the Jews
he's so quiet.*
But us Jews know no quiet.
I had it wrong all along.
He says, *He's not as bad as Waters*, meaning Roger,
which gets me upset
because how can you measure an antisemite in quarter notes?
If one says *Kike*
and the other one convulses when they hear your last name, Lippman,
what's the difference?
In my experience, most Rosh Hashanas, Eno is quieter than Waters.
Most Ma'arivs you couldn't locate an Eno drumbeat but a Waters' bass line,
it's right there beside the Torah trying to burn down the alphabet.
Music for Airports will shut you down in a way that *Echoes* won't.
See, homeostasis is everything when it comes to survival.
And I don't know what to do with myself,
if it is true what Mark tells me.
I stopped listening to The Floyd a few years back.
But Eno. I don't know if I could bring myself to cut him out of the daily
    sonic experience.
Homeostatic dissonance is a funny thing
because they came for us on 10/7
and the internal metronome has reset
and maybe that's what King of the Jews has been all along: homeostasis.
Don't matter how many antisemites throw their grenades at our heads,
jump the kibbutz walls,
turn down their synthesizers really low.
The trick is: don't let them lull you to sleep.
Don't let them seduce you with their whiny guitar solos
trying to convince you they are not dressed up as murderers.

Shalom My Dears

Every morning, I come around the turn on I-90 towards Natick
and there's this red tree that illuminates the green trees
right there in the middle of the autumnal hill.
It turned sooner than the rest and I shout, *You bastard*,
because what else can I do when I am supposed to see God in its leaves?
I do, see God, and it's not any God,
it's King of the Jews God, my God, our God,
and for the first time in my life, I am not afraid to say
or crash my car
or turn my face
from it.
For the first time in my life, I am ready to die inside of it—
that red tree of my God on a hill of green trees
that could also be my peoples' God
but as the metaphor goes, is not.

Earlier this morning I sat in a classroom and was the only Jew.
I said, *Hey, I'm the only Jew*, and the students looked at me
like I was the only Jew.
I said, *Now we read Maus*, with a German accent to make the walls fall down.
I said, *Who knows what The Holocaust is?*
There was such a silence from the abyss I said, *Ach*, it was a silence of hysteria.
The hysteria of not knowing and being ashamed.
It was a field of green trees not knowing
and me and my red tree King of the Jews God
surrounded *Am Israel Chai* with all of our arms
and they looked at me like I was an ogre from the west side of Manhattan—
94th and Central Park West right after the war, any war,
but it's not their fault, right, it's never anybody else's fault?

So, I rose from my chair and left, said, *Shalom my dears*,
got in my car and drove to my red tree on the green hill
to be with my people
even though there was nowhere left to park and all the cars had already
   crashed.

Bread-Of-Affliction Is King of the Jews

Yesterday in Wegmans I ran into the rabbi.
Not my rabbi. Just the rabbi. Rabbi Beker.
We used to work together at Maimonides,
the modern orthodox school down the road.
So many carrots, I said.
He said, *My wife*,
and we didn't have to say anything else,
two days before Pesach, before matzoh and Miriam's cup
and Elijah and the endless bread-of-affliction crumbs
you find curled up in your ear
after the last seder is done.
We miss you, he said. I said, *It was the money*
and I wanted to bum-rush the gum aisle
because it's always the money
and I am tired of the money
and maybe if I were more of the rabbi I could be
then I wouldn't have left Maimonides to work with the goyim
who have no idea what *chag pesach sameach* means
or even what a Jew is.
That's why at the end of 2nd period I stand on my desk and scream,
The bread-of-affliction is King of the Jews part 1 and part 2 is everything else,
and everyone laughs in horror or joy or sorrow or disease
because this year will never be like last year
when we open the door for Elijah
and it will be exactly the same.

The Only Sound of Feeling Good About Something in the Distance

I can't stop seeing the opening shot of *The Boy*.
That small film by Yahva Winner who got cut down on 10/7.
What's it like to make the opening shot
a shot
   of an abundant wheatfield that disappears into Gaza?
I want to feel good about *The Boy* and about the students who don't know
what The Holocaust is and L'Shana Tova
but they killed Yahva Winner
who saved his family,
got in the way of all those guns and missiles and bombs and bad words
and saved his family.
His last film is his last film is our first day
is his present to the birthday of 10/7.
You see, I want to feel good about something
but in the opening shot of *The Boy* there is a field at dusk
and a waterspout that gets bigger and bigger and goes higher and higher
and you can hear the wind and the sound of distant explosions and
   gunshots
and the irrigation spout is broken
and the water is wasted and it shoots higher and higher and hopefully, one
   day,
the sound it makes will be the only sound of feeling good
about something in the distance
of the memory of Yahva Winner
may his memory be there for a blessing.

Sweet Talkin' King Jew

That's me, I'm the Jew in *Maus*.
I'm the fucking disheveled Jew in Sandler's *The Cobbler*.
I am that guy in a plum and a toothbrush.
I am the Hebrew at Maimonides who does not daven,
knows not the prayers, teaches the kids *Night*.
When I taught *Night*, I didn't teach *Night*.
Wiesel was the Jew, and we read his words, together, all of us Jews,
to feel the words in our lungs and teeth
and when I go to the New York Bagel Factory off of route 9
I am the only sweet talkin' Jew
and there are no other Jews for miles around,
and cities and countries around.
There are no Jewish mountains even though every mountain has the blood
   of my siblings spilled across its trees and leaves and dead mosquitoes.
I am the Jew mosquito and the Jew butcher and Jew poet
and the physicist Jew.
And so are my kids and your kids
but when I am alone, I am always alone;
I have never been more alone in my Jew then now,
the Jew in *Maus* and out of *Maus*
and on the road that leads to Jerusalem and Gaza and Thetford and Iowa
   City and Brooklyn, oh God Brooklyn, Bubbie,
where are you now?
Where have you gone you big breasted Jew
who never sat in synagogue, so I sit in synagogue with all my Jews for you.
With all the Jews who will never be mine and will always be mine
and everyone else's
because I made a friend once, Barak,
who couldn't speak for a month
and then said, *I lost 25 brothers on October 7th,*
when he drove me to the mechanic
because I didn't have a ride to pick up my broken car;
he was my ride;
can you even imagine that number, 25?

But Inside the Rain

This is why I hate reading:
Israeli Woman Kidnapped and Killed by Hamas in Inhumane Conditions.
And I'm like *fuck you*
But don't even know who I am talking to
because it could be Hamas or the Israelis or Bibi or the IDF or the bunny on the lawn
that has nowhere to go in the rain
but inside the rain.
And I think of Eden Yerushalmi inside one of those tunnels,
inside the darkness in the filth in the circle of murderers who stink like murderers
and filth
and this is why I hate reading.
Because how do you stay inside that?
Because I have to imagine staying inside those words
and that's when I really know that I'm telling myself *fuck you*
because how dare I sit on this couch
with this dog
in this breeze
in this light
steps from the fridge that is filled
with strawberries and steak
that I can get inside of any time I want?
Because what am I supposed to do when Eden Yerushalmi was King of the Jews
for 11 months in the darkness and then they cut her down?
11 mos. inside the inhumane darkness.
I don't think I will ever read that word again, *inhumane*,
and not think of Eden Yerushalmi whose sisters, Shani and May, said,
They starved her before they murdered her.

DOUBLE CHAI

Chai Everlasting

This morning Charles Mingus was King of the Jews.
He didn't even know it.
He's been dead 400 years.
But when *Better Get Hit In Your Soul* came on the radio
you knew things were about to fall out of the sky.
And then they fell out of the sky
and you couldn't name them
but you could name them.
Maybe they were words like *forgiveness* and *ricochet*.
Maybe they were letters like aleph and gimel.
You were in your car, and he just came out of you, Mingus,
and when he did, you knew you were done for
and had one job. To listen.
You didn't even have to listen to *Better Get Hit In Your Soul*
to know that this was the divine intervention of chai everlasting.
Just listen to everything everywhere all the time.
Mingus' bass playing told you so,
but it wasn't even that
because when Booker Ervin's tenor hit you in the chest
there it was—the opening of The Red Sea
right there on Washington Street
and for a second, everybody was free
because there was no more bottom
and there had never been one to begin with.

Revelation Pants

I walked Autumn through the neighborhood on a leash
that I wanted to cut.
To set her free in her freedom pants.
Isn't that the whole slide-down-the-water-slide thing?
To be free in our living room pants or our jumping jack pants?
I walked her and I was free in my dungaree pants
thinking: *Genevieve is King of the Jews.*
That's freedom right there.
To be King of the Jews.
You know you are in your rabbi pants but not because you are a rabbi
and what does that mean to have rabbi pants?
Is that the freedom of the diaspora crammed into a synagogue saying magical words
for a congregation that is in dire need of a revelation?
I can't imagine putting on those burden pants.
Those: I gotta put on my Give Them A Revelation Pants.
What I can imagine is you on your surfboard in your ocean
in your wet suit pants as a freedom beyond what the waves can tell you.
And once you mentioned Franz Rosenzweig and I have no idea who he is,
so I look him up and there it is: *Baden-Baden.*
And I'm like, that sounds like a brand for some new slick chinos.
Hey, honey, where you going?
I'm going to The Gap, babe, to get me a new pair of Baden-Baden.
Those soft cotton slacks to make me look like a million bucks.
Until I read that Baden-Baden is a series of symposia to make contemporary culture
into the object of historical contemplation and I need you, Genevieve, King of us Hebrews,
to tell me what the fuck that means.
That's unfair though.
That's not freedom though.
That's not the way it's supposed to go, though.
Because the world is not yours and you are not the world
for anyone but the kingdom of your own heart
even when you are up there on the bima
and all your progressive hippie culture divergent congregants

are wondering about your rabbi pants and your homecooking pants and
 the pants you hang
to dry on your line
when solitude is the only thing that you really want.
To put on your solitude pants and answer no questions from the world,
have no questions of your own to ponder.
You just want the wind, to feel the wind,
because what you know as King of the Jews
is that the best breeze is the breeze that has no pants
and who needs 'em anyway
to walk down the street at lunchtime, through Time Square and not give a
 fuck in the world what anyone thinks or has to say.

Golf Jews

What's synagogue?
some blonde-haired 8th grader asked me,
and I said, *It's a place where Jews go to die*, and then I said, *Oops, to pray*,
and he said, *Cool.*
I was driving the golf team back to school from the golf range because I'm the golf coach
in the white school bus
and it was coming on Shabbos, and I thought, *I have to explain?*
I got so tired thinking *I have to explain* that I crashed the bus into a phone pole
but no one got hurt.
We all just sat on the side of the road
scattered with pitching wedges, three irons, 1 wood, Titleist balls,
and watched the white bus burn.
Mr. Lippman, the blonde-haired 8th grade boy asked,
are you okay?
and he was King of the Jews for not knowing.
Declan, I asked, *you really don't know what a synagogue is?*
And he said, *It's like this,* he said, *right here,*
because I prayed we wouldn't die when you fell asleep at the wheel
and God didn't let us die
and I got mad at myself for being so tired
of having to explain myself
but I guess it doesn't matter what kind of God you believe in,
what you call God,
God just does God shit when 13-year-olds make prayers
that we don't die
and we don't die
and then he calls it *synagogue*
after saying, *What's synagogue?*

The Köln Concert Is King of the Jews

This is the second time I have listened to The Köln Concert in 2 days.
Keith Jarrett is King of the Jews.
You know why he is King of the Jews?
Because he made up The Köln Concert on stage, like magic, a miracle.
He's King of the Jews because Jarrett is a piano player
who can't use his hands anymore.
They took away his hands,
the God of all things.
I listen to The Köln Concert, so I won't ever forget what it's like
that he made it up on the spot,
on a piano he didn't even want
that fell out of the sky.
This is why David says to me,
Forgetting is TGP worthy
because it's an avatar of death,
in an email and if David and Keith Jarrett had a baby
it would be the end of forgetting,
which means that no one would die
and even if they did
there would always be music.
That's why King of the Jews is a musician,
to make sure we don't forget our stories
even when we have dementia or the onslaught of Alzheimer's—
we don't forget the dirty desert that made us people.
That's why I listen to The Köln Concert 2 times in 2 days.
To remember that we are all people, and we must not forget
that part close to 6 minutes inside the music—
you can feel him getting somewhere, Jarrett.
He's remembering everything for everyone,
working out his notes so we don't forget
and he knows that this is his job,
and then he plays that low note from the left hand that shouldn't be there
    but is exactly where it's supposed to be,
it's the small trickle of whatever holy water that will never die
and he's almost there but he retreats and then,
somewhere close to 7 and a half minutes, he's done it,

not just parted the waters
but moved through all the seas in the world without the part.
It's all those chords and he's moaning along with them in some rocking chair
gut harmony and that's when you realize
that David is not King of the Jews
and Keith is not either,
it's the piano,
it's not even the piano,
it's The Köln Concert that will kill us every time
even though we won't ever forget what happens the third time we hear it.

Not That Kind of Jew

When they launch the missiles into Tel Aviv
and I'm in my rich school all I want to do is be at my old poor school.
That's the school called Maimonides with the ceilings that leak when it rains
and the sticky floors and broken desks.
It's filled with Jews and Jews that are Modern Orthodox Jews
and I'm not that kind of Jew
but when I ask my wife,
Are you going to be okay in front of your congregation that is Reform
as a Conservative Jew?
she says, *It doesn't matter now, who gives a fuck*
and I've always felt like if they came for us, asked us for our papers,
took our silver and gold and borscht and siddurim
it would not matter where you plant your feet
in what synagogue
at what hour
to daven for the heart of the world.
That's always been the yellow light to follow—to pray
for the heart of the world.
Today, there are missiles over Tel Aviv
and I want to quit this job at this fancy school and go home to my Maimonides
so I can sleep under the leaky roof with my brothers and sisters
with whom I share nothing
but who saved my life
even if there are missiles overhead sent to blow our brains to smithereens
all over the sticky floors.

King of the Jews in His Joy

I wanted to ask Alexander Lobanov what it was like to make the best Old Fashion
because I had a dream that he knew the answer.
But I couldn't ask him.
They killed him with a bullet.
Hamas took him from his martini glasses and his bourbon at the Nova Festival
and then he lived in a tunnel for 11 months
and when he was there while he was there
his son was born and so that makes his son King of the Jews
and it makes the best Old Fashions King of the Jews
and it makes Alex the king of bourbon and I wonder
when Netanyahu met with his mother to say we ask for your forgiveness
if she said *you dumb man*
in English or Hebrew
or if she said nothing,
just picked up her grandson, turned her back,
and wandered into the park to let the child crawl in the dirt.
All day long, the only thing I have wanted to do
is bring her an Old Fashion and say:
Alex taught me how to make this in my dreams for you
when he was being King of the Jews in his joy
for all the dancers who danced in the desert
and knew only love.

Juan Is the King Sauce of Peace

Juan was always my king
and I was his king
and we were so far apart as Mexican and Jew
but had colors to toss back and forth like pecans.
Some days he had the purple and I had the orange.
Some days the yellow came out of his fingers and the blue came out of mine.
Once we had a conversation about kindness.
He said, *Let's do a kindness project.*
I said, *You are the kindest king I know.*
It was weird to me after,
like a tree or a mushroom is weird,
that we had to do a kindness project.
Kindness should just be kindness
without having to be a project.
I will help you across the street with your broken knee.
You will help me plant an orange tree when my back is busted.
That's peace.
That's the sauce of peace.
Juan is the sauce of peace
and today he's King of Jews when tomorrow he'll be King of the Chicanos
and after that, the King of the oregano and cilantro and eggplant.
It's good to have kings in your life
that are so far apart from you.
That's what he taught me and he'll tell you that I taught him the same thing.
But see, that's just him just being kind
and the world owes him a lot in his colors and words and fedoras and plaid
    shirts.
They named a school after him in his hometown for all the kids.
When he's long gone
his Technicolor breath will touch the tops of their heads
and no one will get hurt.

Like Oranges and Holy Land

My wife is King of the Jews because she's a rabbi
and she has to get up in front of 200 people and talk about sweetness and apples
and 613 mitzvot
and she can't travel to Israel where today a 22-year-old squad commander in the IDF
can't have any kind of sweet new year with his face in the dust.
He was killed.
We are all killed.
When Rachel goes up to the bima to say the Shehechiyanu she is killed, too,
and no one can go to Haifa or Paris
with apples and honey dripping off of their fingertips
but we have to no matter.
We have to go for the family of the 22-year-old squad commander killed
and everyone else who has died fighting for something they believe in
like oranges
and holy land
and the presence of mind to live free in a way that makes most sense to them.
It seems so simple no matter the holiday and today we are killed
out of our living
to get closer to our breath
so we can travel into our solitude
and pretend we know something, but we don't.
We know nothing
and tonight my wife will move to the bima and travel with her pain
and her love and her joy
and her tears and her Torah.
She will stand before her people, and she will be King of the Jews for a second
or a minute or an eon
and we will dip our apples in our honey with her
and move with her
through the force of her
into the grief of the 22-year-old IDF squad commander's family
so his memory might be a blessing
in a new year of sweetness and horror
and doing kind things for anyone who believes we can't.

Crush the Half Notes So Holy

Homelessness is King of the Jews
like a piano is king of the world
and what's the image?
The soldier with blood and dirt on their face
comes upon a busted Steinway in the middle of the rubble
and plays Beethoven or Brahams
and you think, *ah fuck, humanity,*
but where is our home?
Us Jews?

The homelessness of a people is the earth they try to live on
when no one wants you to live on it.
What's the image?
The piano falls out of the sky
and is obliterated
but there is the Jew who picks up the pieces in their wandering
to play Monk or Rachmaninoff
to get themselves home.

But homelessness is King of the Jews
like a piano is king of the world
and here is the image.
A piano in the pocket.
Because no matter where you find yourself,
lost and wayward,
there has to be a piano in your pocket
so you can pull it out under the bridge,
tucked in the tunnel,
praying in the penthouse,
and bang the keys,

smash the keys so loud
to remind everyone that you belong, Jew,
that you have a place to pray;

crush those half notes so holy
the world has to listen
even if it hates your guts for all eternity.

Shofar Party

When Jill gets up in front of a 500 people at the school meeting in the fancy
    theater
and reads the book about Yom Kippur that's a children's book—
it's the Big Bad Wolf story reimagined with a shofar and teshuvah
and fasting and breaking the fast—
she is King of the Jews.
There are 500 people in the school and I'm the fifth Jew of 5 Jews including Jill
so I have to cry for all my people sitting in the theater
and that's what I do, I cry for my people
or maybe I am crying for myself
or for Jill
or for the wolf of the world that has tried to eat us for ages.
The one who eats the pigs and the Jews and the broken and the bored.
The children's book is a book about Yom Kippur and there are pigs in the story
but in this story the wolf helps the pigs
because he is being his best self and repenting
and he doesn't even know the word *teshuvah*
like the kids at the school don't know what a shofar is
so that's when I get up in my tears
in the theater with the velvet seats and big chandelier
where Jill is King of the Hebrew nation.
I stand up in my tears and pull the shofar out of my pocket and yell *Tekiah*
and then I blow it, I blast it, I howl it
like the shofar is my Torah
and Jill is my King.
I blow it and blow it and then Jill takes out her shofar,
the one she conjures out of midair because she's a magician of the light,
and she blows hers
and we are blowing it together and the wolf disappears
and all the children's books disappear
and then the weirdest thing happens.
The 495 other people in the theater grab their shofars from their backpacks
and blue blazers and eyeballs and their bones
and they start blowing and blasting and belching.
It's a shofar party and I can't believe it, how Jill made it,
but, I guess, that's what kings do.
They make people see what their best selves can be

and then, at least for a second,
we are all our best selves,
we are all teshuvah and that's when someone yells, *tekiah gedolah*,
and we all blow together,
one big, long shofar blast that I swear, three months from now,
the whole world can still hear.

Danielle Haim Is King of the Jews

Danielle Haim is King of the Jews when she sings on Bon Iver's record,
If Only I Could Wait
but only when she sings *Northern Lights*
and her voice goes into some harmonic skyway of the otherworld.
I want to say that Alana Haim and Estie Haim and Haim
are king of the Jews and that's because they are Jews and I don't like leaving
 anyone out.
But sometimes Justin Vernon is the king
because his falsetto up against a flock of starlings
is some velvet edged walkway of this world
smashed up inside that world
you can't ever talk about.
Except that I can't stop thinking of Danielle on a motorbike at the ocean
trying to split the ocean
in this season of anti-Jewishness
like there was ever a season of pro-love Jewishness.
If you don't know what I am talking about, fuck off.
If you don't know what I am talking about know this: all the Haim sisters are
 Jews
and somewhere back in time
one of their ancestors lived in shtetl fifty miles from Prague
and got sad most days
because there was someone always coming for them.
That's why Mr. Vernon is king of the sounds,
all of the sounds, in the service of sadness and music
and says, *I am the luckiest man in the world*, but Danielle is the luckiest man in
 the world
in the service of her spirit and today I give it to her, the title *king*,
when she sings *If Only I Could Wait*,
into a possibility of love
that is Vernon's baritone,
an alien culture of surprise and anticipation
that every time you hear the song,
her voice in the low registers,
there she is, at the ocean,
splitting the sea like it needs to be split every day
and Moses, that other king had it wrong
because he only did it once.

Your Sunflower Field Life

When you go to the dance festival that's all you're supposed to do.
Move your feet. Shake your ass. Sweat your face off.
When Ori Danino went to The Nova Festival
all he wanted to do was move his feet, shake his ass, sweat his face off.
I imagine he did that.
I imagine he smiled for a long time and drank a lot of water.
I have never been to a dance festival. I have been to a bluegrass festival.
Everyone there moved their banjo feet.
Shook their mandolin ass.
Sweat their face off yellow
like a sunflower field in summer.
If I didn't know that Ori Danino was from Jerusalem
I would have thought that he might have been half Jew, half Italian.
Danino. Stromboli. Ciao bello. Shalom.
When Ori Danino went to the Nova Dance Festival in October,
I am sure all he thought about was the beginning of his life.
If you are that young
that's all you do
till you are 32.
You think that every day is the beginning of your life.
Is the beginning of your sunflower field life
and that no matter how Jewish or Italian or Polish or Palestinian or
    Russian you are,
you glisten.
That's what happens at festivals because there is so much smiling.
And the next time you are at one, the sunflower field festival,
put your face into one of those big yellow prickly flowers,
get your nose deep in there and say his name, Ori Danino,
till you make sure you can hear the sunflower say it back.

We Bow to the Floor to Pray

There is this part in the Rosh Hashana service, during *Aleinu*,
where we all get down on the floor to pray and utter, mutter, manifest:
Aleinu leshabei'ach,
It is upon us.
We bow to the floor to pray
but we really get our whole bodies on the floor
and let the dirt ruin our pretty clothes
that most definitely should be ruined.
The old people in the shul in the old days in olden desert times
didn't give a shit about what they wore to synagogue
because synagogue
wasn't about white shirts and Joseph Aboud sport coats.
It was about saying *what's up god*
I am going to get sealed in the book of life
and be a better person this year than I was last year.
All that King of the Jews beautiful bullshit.
But what I really want to say is:
that we get down on the floor and lately
when I'm down there,
really down there,
that's where all the trees are
and all the minds are being mindful;
and when I am really down inside that floor—
which means we are nothing in this world if we don't get dirty—
that's when the whole purpose of the King of the Jews makes sense.
To get dirty in the trees and lose the mind.
And there we all are, us Jews, on the floor of the holy house,
some of us wanting to get up,
some of wanting to be filthy for the rest of our lives.

Led Zeppelin Is King of the Jews on Kol Nidre

What if Led Zeppelin played *Kol Nidre* tonight?
In all the synagogues across the world?
They could do it in the spirit of *Goin' To California*
or they could do it like *Ramble On*.
Just a bunch of old rockers taking us into atonement.
John Paul Jones on mandolin.
Robert humming in his big balled blue jeans.
Jimmy with a lute and Bonham, from the dead,
scratching brushes across the snare hide.
It'd be some kind of mystical, magical hallucination of sorrow.
I bet it would bring the world together
even if you hate the Jews
but found yourself walking by Temple Beth Zion on Beacon
or floating towards El Transito Synagogue in the town of Toledo
where auto-de-fe was all the rage back in the day.
The music turning you inside out into forgiveness.
The sky some abundant space of flight to miss.
The way you start to think of Neilah and not because the fast is almost
 over
the bagels are on the way
but because you've been through something,
you've gone inside the hunger to obliterate desire.
And with no more desire
there is just the body and then the body disappears
and the words follow and there is only, what's left, the shofar—
Robert Plant, his mouth on the ram's horn,
with his big lungs,
closing the gate.

King of the Jews

She Was Queen of the County and the King of Love

Once I had a student named Ahava.
I didn't know what her name meant.
She was queen of the county and the king of love.
That's what *ahava* means, *love*.
Once we had a fight. I am not supposed to get into fights with students,
but Ahava said mean things to kids
and I said, *No no no, no means things to kids.*
Ahava called me *puta* in Spanish
and I didn't even know she spoke Spanish or knew how to curse in Spanish.
Once she stormed out of room and I yelled back *puta* but I didn't really.
What I wanted to do, really, was forget that there was meanness in the world.
Ahava was fun to teach.
She knew how space worked.
Mr. Lippman, she once said,
that big red thing on Jupiter, The Great Red Storm,
it's been swirling for 180 years at 420 miles an hour
and sometimes it moves
even though the astronomers and astrophysicists don't know anything,
and thank God because that thing
is like my life.
Once, Ahava told me I was her favorite teacher even though I called her *puta*.
That's why you are my favorite teacher.
Ahava can read your mind, so be careful.
That's what I learned as her teacher. The kids can read your mind.
Once upon a time she was queen of the county and the king of love.
I am convinced she still is.
For many years I have always ended every class by saying
to the kids as they shuffled out of the door, *Peace and Love.*
Once, Ahava left the classroom and said, *Mr. Lippman, Shalom ve'ahava.*
That's for you, she said.
That's for everyone.
Then she went into the hallway, The Great Red Storm,
and gave everyone the middle finger like show owned all the planets.

Form Follows Function Is King

There is only one version of Cohen's *Hallelujah*—
it's Buckley doing it live at Sin-e.
Back in the early 90s before any of us were born.
The melody was born long before that
and it will be around before any of us are alive again.
And they use it in synagogue, Psalm 150, like it was there forever.
He wrote it in a dark room on a napkin on a floorboard
like it was always there, the melody, and who knows if there was a woman
    bathing
on the roof or someone with rope to tie you to a kitchen chair
with the blazing knives, the submerged ark?
It's an ancient thing, that melody,
and he must have snatched it out of Exodus
when the Jews were on foot, fleeing, or from breath of God.
How do you get so lucky?
You work hard, that's how;
you write your face off in dark rooms with low wattage and then forget about it
until someone like Jeff comes along and plays it over and over in his dark room
then performs it to no one.
I sat in synagogue, and they sang Psalm 150 and there was Cohen's ancient
    melody.
I was looking out the window at the autumn trees and I knew where God was.
Out there in the crashing of cymbals.
In the crashing red leaves against yellow leaves and Jeff is dead and so is
    Leonard
but the melody, there from the beginning, from all beginnings, was not,
perfectly rendered to fit the word.
A thing so right with another thing there is no talking except for Buckley,
at the end of his set,
4 people in the room:
Good night. I love you so much.
You're fabulous.
Beautiful.
And I love you.
And that's all, man.
Let's go drink
and sleep.

The Sukkah Is King of the Jews

The sukkah is King of the Jews
because you eat in it together, chicken and eggplant.
You sit and are shaded from the sun with the lulav as your left hand
and the lulav as your whole body.
All the people come over and sit
and there is sun and sometimes it rains.
You are with your kings and you talk about fire and special things
like weddings and pain.
Once, you built a sukkah and it was 10/7
and once you built a sukkah and it was your daughter's birthday.
The thing about the sukkah is that it is the king of everything
because you have harvested the food
and when you harvest the food
you give it to other people so other people can eat the corn and the tomatoes
and it has nothing to do with you.
This year you can lie in the sukkah and see the Northern Lights.
They are for no one.
They are the glistening crown on the tips of the s'cach.
The last time you built a sukkah
you knew nothing about kings and Jews.
Today when you built the sukkah
you built it in the rain.
The Northern Lights were crying
but you could not see their colors.
You could imagine them, though,
and there was enough food for all the people.

King of the Jews Is One Word

Almog help me.
He went to help Shahar because Shahar needed to be helped
and when you care about the person you love
you help them.
But there was nothing Almog could do
but be taken
and he was taken
and there was nothing Shahar could do, and she was not saved.
There are so many stories, there are too many stories.
Then you choose to remember what you need to remember
to live laughing into your life.
I choose to remember Almog with his face
close to Shahar's face
dangling in the hot sun
before she was not saved, and he was taken.
Shahar, hold my hand.
Shahar, take my hand.
But she could not speak because there are no words.
There are too many words
and there are too many stories and what are the words?
There are no more words, Almog.
There is only one word.
It is *levov.*

Will You Help with These Sheets Please
(for Rachel)

I can't even write this poem, so I make the bed.
Throw the covers across the mattress like it's a storm waiting to unleash its
 fury.
Then he gets off his trumpet and says, *These songs came to me right after
 10/7,*
and the blankets burn my hands
but that's when I start to cry.
Help me with these pillows,
I say to the Japanese lady sitting next to me at the little table at the jazz
 show.
She's with her 10-year-old son and Cohen picks up the flute and says,
We have to stand inside the complexity not beside it,
which is when the music starts, and my crying begins,
Barak Mori's fingers up and down the standup bass
because he's running fast.
The music is running fast and the bed stands still.
There is so much stillness in the cherry wood I can't write this poem.
I have to be with the stillness and Avishai picks up the trumpet.
The music runs and it's the kids at the music festival running fast
through the bullets and into the bullets and beyond the bullets.
Will you help me with the sheets? I ask the Japanese mom's kid?
He is bouncing up and down to the snare's beat, Ziv Ravitz kicking up
 dessert dust
in Boston,
so far from the Negev
you couldn't see straight if you wanted.
I wanted.
I want to put my head between the pillows to suck up all the world's tears.
There are so many of them that someone is drowning far away
and there are no life jackets to quiet the horn.
It's quiet now.
It's the stricken and robust grief of the end of a song
so we throw torn blankets
across the wind to stop it from blowing.
We have to get inside of it, Cohen says,
to reach the somewhere else.

It's right here as the melody gets softer and softer
that the dead will never forget to remind us to make the bed.
They are so far away we have made them our tears.
Cohen's tattoo is a tear, too.
It's a branch that drips down his neck from behind his ear.
It's a ladder of joy.
When I wrote this record, he tells us, *I was trying to make the bed
but the massacre was too close so I wrote it anyway.*
And I can't write this poem because the headboard is too soft, too blue velvet,
so I smooth the top sheet over the bottom sheet
but there's always a wrinkle and the dog jumps onto the mattress to sully up
   the cotton.
I will help you, the Japanese boy says, and shakes out the kinks
still in rhythm with Yonathan's scales, his left hand barely moving,
his right, its own kind of ram's horn to summon the sweet.
Maybe, I think, we need the rest of the world more than ever to smooth out
   the shakes
and that's why we need more trumpets and trumpeters.
And I still can't write this poem given how many tears there are in my face,
given what I know and what I don't know about taking a nap.
I cried for an hour inside the music.
That's how Jewish I am, inside the music.
That's how Hungarian and Polish I am.
That's how Japanese I am, beside the music.
My daughter wrote this next piece, Avishai tells us, *that's how quiet she is,*
and someone responds, *What about her royalties?*
and the whole room laughs
and the Japanese woman looks at my tissues and grabs my hand, but she
   doesn't really,
I only imagine Rachel close to the music with me,
screaming in my mind, *Rachel Rachel Rachel,*
because she should be here
fluffing up the pillows so we can settle in together for the night,
a flock of trumpets flying overhead,
our naked feet touching beneath the quilt,
the tears all dried up,
never dried up,
which is why I can't write this poem,
which is why this poem should never have been written.

Acknowledgements:

Some of these poems have been previously published in *Image, Judith Magazine, On Being Jewish,* and *The American Poetry Review.*

About the Author

Matthew Lippman is the author of 7 poetry collections. His latest collection, *We Are All Sleeping With Our Sneakers On* (2024), is published by Four Way Books. His previous collection *Mesmerizingly Sadly Beautiful* (2020) is published by Four Way Books. It was the recipient of the 2018 Levis Prize. In 2027 his next collection, *Cry Baby Cry*, will be published by Four Way Books. He lives in Boston where he teaches English Literature and Creative Writing.

The Jewish Poetry Project

jpoetry.us

Ben Yehuda Press

From the Coffee House of Jewish Dreamers: Poems of Wonder and Wandering and the Weekly Torah Portion by Isidore Century

"Isidore Century is a wonderful poet. His poems are funny, deeply observed, without pretension." —*The Jewish Week*

The House at the Center of the World: Poetic Midrash on Sacred Space by Abe Mezrich

"Direct and accessible, Mezrich's midrashic poems often tease profound meaning out of his chosen Torah texts. These poems remind us that our Creator is forgiving, that the spiritual and physical can inform one another, and that the supernatural can be carried into the everyday."
—Yehoshua November, author of *God's Optimism*

we who desire:
Poems and Torah riffs by Sue Swartz

"Sue Swartz does magnificent acrobatics with the Torah. She takes the English that's become staid and boring, and adds something that's new and strange and exciting. These are poems that leave a taste in your mouth, and you walk away from them thinking, what did I just read? Oh, yeah. It's the Bible."
—Matthue Roth, author, *Yom Kippur A Go-Go*

Open My Lips: Prayers and Poems by Rachel Barenblat

"Barenblat's God is a personal God—one who lets her cry on His shoulder, and who rocks her like a colicky baby. These poems bridge the gap between the ineffable and the human. This collection will bring comfort to those with a religion of their own, as well as those seeking a relationship with some kind of higher power."
—Satya Robyn, author, *The Most Beautiful Thing*

Words for Blessing the World: Poems in Hebrew and English by Herbert J. Levine

"These writings express a profoundly earth-based theology in a language that is clear and comprehensible. These are works to study and learn from."
—Rodger Kamenetz, author, *The Jew in the Lotus*

Shiva Moon: Poems by Maxine Silverman

"The poems, deeply felt, are spare, spoken in a quiet but compelling voice, as if we were listening in to her inner life. This book is a precious record of the transformation saying Kaddish can bring. It deserves to be read."
—Howard Schwartz, author, *The Library of Dreams*

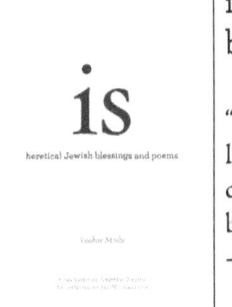

is: heretical Jewish blessings and poems by Yaakov Moshe (Jay Michaelson)

"Finally, Torah that speaks to and through the lives we are actually living: expanding the tent of holiness to embrace what has been cast out, elevating what has been kept down, advancing what has been held back, reveling in questions, revealing contradictions."
—Eden Pearlstein, aka eprhyme

Texts to the Holy: Poems
by Rachel Barenblat

"These poems are remarkable, radiating a love of God that is full bodied, innocent, raw, pulsating, hot, drunk. I can hardly fathom their faith but am grateful for the vistas they open. I will sit with them, and invite you to do the same."
—Merle Feld, author of *A Spiritual Life*

The Sabbath Bee: Love Songs to Shabbat
by Wilhelmina Gottschalk

"Torah, say our sages, has seventy faces. As these prose poems reveal, so too does Shabbat. Here we meet Shabbat as familiar housemate, as the child whose presence transforms a family, as a spreading tree, as an annoying friend who insists on being celebrated, as a woman, as a man, as a bee, as the ocean."
—Rachel Barenblat, author, *The Velveteen Rabbi's Haggadah*

All the Holes Line Up: Poems and Translations
by Zackary Sholem Berger

"Spare and precise, Berger's poems gaze unflinchingly at—but also celebrate—human imperfection in its many forms. And what a delight that Berger also includes in this collection a handful of his resonant translations of some of the great Yiddish poets."
—Yehoshua November, author of *God's Optimism* and *Two Worlds Exist*

How to Bless the New Moon:
Songs of the Sovereign and the Icon
by Rachel Kann

"Rachel Kann is a master wordsmith. Her poems are rich in content, packed with life's wisdom and imbued with soul. May this collection of her work enable more of the world to enjoy her offerings."
—Sarah Yehudit Schneider, author of *You Are What You Hate*

Into My Garden: Prayers
by David Caplan

"The beauty of Caplan's book is that it is not polemical. It does not set out to win an argument or ask you whether you've put your tefillin on today. These gentle poems invite the reader into one person's profound, ambiguous religious experience."
—*The Jewish Review of Books*

Between the Mountain and the Land is the Lesson: Poetic Midrash on Sacred Community by Abe Mezrich

"Abe Mezrich cuts straight back to the roots of the Midrashic tradition, sermonizing as a poet, rather than ideologue. Best of all, Abe knows how to ask questions and avoid the obvious answers."
—Jake Marmer, author, *Jazz Talmud*

NOKADDISH: Poems in the Void
by Hanoch Guy Kaner

"A subversive, midrashic play with meanings–specifically Jewish meanings, and then the reversal and negation of these meanings."
—Robert G. Margolis

An Added Soul: Poems for a New Old Religion
by Herbert J. Levine

"Herbert J. Levine's lovely poems swing wide the double doors of English and Hebrew and open on the awe of being. Clear and direct, at ease in both tongues, these lyrics embrace a holiness unyoked from myth and theistic searching."
—Lynn Levin, author, *The Minor Virtues*

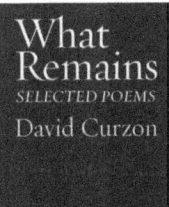

What Remains
by David Curzon

"Aphoristic, ekphrastic, and precise revelations animate WHAT REMAINS. In his stunning rewriting of Psalm 1 and other biblical passages, Curzon shows himself to be a fabricator, a collector, and an heir to the literature, arts, and wisdom traditions of the planet."
—Alicia Ostriker, author of *The Volcano and After*

The Shortest Skirt in Shul
by Sass Oron

"These poems exuberantly explore gender, Torah, the masks we wear, and the way our bodies (and the ways we wear them) at once threaten stable narratives, and offer the kind of liberation that saves our lives."
—Alicia Jo Rabins, author of *Divinity School*, composer of *Girls In Trouble*

Walking Triptychs
by Ilya Gutner

These are poems from when I walked about Shanghai and thought about the meaning of the Holocaust.

Book of Failed Salvation
by Julia Knobloch

"These beautiful poems express a tender longing for spiritual, physical, and emotional connection. They detail a life in movement—across distances, faith, love, and doubt."
—David Caplan, author, *Into My Garden*

Daily Blessings: Poems on Tractate Berakhot
by Hillel Broder

"Hillel Broder does not just write poetry about the Talmud; he also draws out the Talmud's poetry, finding lyricism amidst legality and re-setting the Talmud's rich images like precious gems in end-stopped lines of verse."
—Ilana Kurshan, author of *If All the Seas Were Ink*

The Red Door: A dark fairy tale told in poems
by Shawn C. Harris

"THE RED DOOR, like its poet author Shawn C. Harris, transcends genres and identities. It is an exploration in crossing worlds. It brings together poetry and story telling, imagery and life events, spirit and body, the real and the fantastic, Jewish past and Jewish present, to spin one tale." —Einat Wilf, author, *The War of Return*

The Missing Jew: Poems 1976-2022
by Rodger Kamenetz

"How does Rodger Kamenetz manage to have so singular a voice and at the same time precisely encapsulate the world view of an entire generation (also mine) of text-hungry American Jews born in the middle of the twentieth century?"
—Jacqueline Osherow, author, *Ultimatum from Paradise* and *My Lookalike at the Krishna Temple: Poems*

The Matter of Families
by Robert H. Deluty

"Robert Deluty's career-spanning collection of New and Selected poems captures the essence of his work: the power of love, joy, and connection, all tied together with the poet's glorious sense of humor. This book is Deluty's masterpiece."
—Richard M. Berlin, M.D., author of *Freud on My Couch*

There Is No Place Without You
by Maya Bernstein

"Bernstein's poems brim with energy and sound, moving the reader around a world mapped by motherhood, contemplation, religion, and the effects of illness on the body and spirit. Her language is lyrical, delicate, and poised; her lens is lucid and original."
—Anthony Anaxagorou, author of *After the Formalities*

Torah Limericks
by Rhonda Rosenheck

"Rhonda Rosenheck knows the Hebrew Bible, and she knows that it can stand up to the sometimes silly, sometimes snarky, but always insightful scholarship packed into each one of these interpretive jewels."
—Rabbi Hillel Norry

Words for a Dazzling Firmament
by Abe Mezrich

"Mezrich is a cultivated craftsman: interpretively astute, sonically deliberate, and spiritually cunning."

—Zohar Atkins, author of *Nineveh*

Everything Thaws
by R. B. Lemberg

"Full of glacier-sharp truths, and moments revealed between words like bodies beneath melting permafrost. As it becomes increasingly plain how deeply our world is shaped by war and climate change and grief and anger, articulating that shape feels urgent and necessary."
—Ruthanna Emrys, author of *A Half-Built Garden*

Ode to the Dove: *An illustrated, bilingual edition of a Yiddish poem by Abraham Sutzkever*
Zackary Sholem Berger, translator
Liora Ostroff, Illustrator

"An elegant volume for lovers of poetry."
—Justin Cammy, translator of *Sutzkever, From the Vilna Ghetto to Nuremberg: Memoir and Testimony*

Poems for a Cartoon Mouse
by Andrew Burt

"Andrew Burt's poetry magnifies the vanishingly small line between danger and safety. This collection asks whether order is an illusion that veils chaos, or vice-versa, juxtaposing images from the Bible with animated films."
—Ari Shapiro, host of NPR's *All Things Considered*

Old Shul
by Pinny Bulman

"Nostalgia gives way to a tender theology, a softly chuckling illumination from within the heart of/as a beautiful, broken sanctuary, somehow both gritty and fragile, grimy and iridescent – not unlike faith itself."
—Jake Marmer, author of *Cosmic Diaspora*

Feet In L.A., But My Womb Lives In Jerusalem, My Breath In Vermont
by Lori Levy

"Takes my breath away. With no pretense whatsoever, they leap, alive, from the page until this reader felt as if she were living Levy's life. How does the author do it?"
—Mary Jo Balistreri, author of *Still*

Poem Hashavuah
by Lexie Botzum and Jessica Spencer

"This collection illuminates the white fire of the Torah — the ancient and modern literary interpretations that carve out the negative space of the Torah's letters so that they dance before us as joyously as when they were given in fire on Sinai."
—Ilana Kurshan, author of *If All the Seas Were Ink*

Bits and Pieces
by Edward Pomerantz

"A natural dramatist who looks back on his life growing up in Washington Heights in a series of vivid vignettes inspired by his early moviegoing."
—Robert Vas Dias, author of *Poetics Of Still Life: A Collage*

Not Akhmatova
by Noah Berlatsky

"In these poems, Noah Berlatsky approaches the work of Anna Akhmatova—or scrambles off in another direction entirely. Writing under the sign of her name, with her but without trying to become her, Berlatsky gives us Anna in transcreation, in translation."
—Sarah Dowling, author of *Entering Sappho*

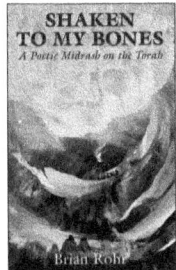

Shaken to My Bones
by Brian Rohr

"In Brian Rohr's exquisite poems, wonders unfold. We are taken along on a journey both ancient and immediate — one that is rewarding beyond comparison."
—Baruch November, author of *Bar Mitzvah Dreams*

So Many Warm Words: Selections from the Poetry of Rosa Nevadovska, translated by Merle L. Bachman

"This bilingual edition makes Nevadovska's oeuvre—poems of loneliness and longing countered by others expressing joyous moments of transcendence—accessible, for the first time, to the English reader."
—Sheva Zucker, editor emerita of *Afn Shvel*.

The Whole Mishpocha
by Philip Terman

"Gathers the Jewish-themed poems of an accomplished poet who has been producing memorable work on the Jewish-American experience for decades. I have long admired Terman's exceptional poems for their Jewish ethos, beautiful lyricism, and emotional risk taking."
—Yehoshua November, author of *God's Optimism*

Styx by Else Lasker-Schüler
translated by Mildred Faintly

"Reborn in Mildred Faintly's magnificent translation, Else Lasker-Schüler's STYX overflows with shudders of desolation, moans of sexual pleasure, ecstatic fusions of love and despite that exalt and torture in equal measure."
—Joy Ladin, author of *The Book of Anna* and *Shekhinah Speaks.*

Chrysalis Summer
by Suzanne Brody

"We are invited into the thoughts and emotions of one woman who plays many roles—teacher, mother, rabbi, and artist. Topics stretch from the mundane business of cleaning up students' glitter to weightier topics such as egalitarianism and Biblical texts."
—Dori Weinstein, author of the *YaYa & YoYo* series *Considered*

Blessed Are You, Wondrous Universe:
A Siddur for Seekers by Herbert J. Levine

"Herb Levine has fashioned a sparkling collection of prayers for a thinking, feeling modern person who wants to express gratitude for the wonder of existence."
—Daniel Matt, translator of the Zohar, author of *God and the Big Bang*, *The Essential Kabbalah*, and *Becoming Elijah*

Animals are Shouting Down from the Sky
by Genevieve Greinetz

"Often heart-stopping, these poems abound in images uniquely unfamiliar. Not intended for the casual reader, they capture the violation of nature, free speech silenced, humanity flattened, families – and friends – failing as they often do."
—Merle Feld, author of *Longing, Poems for a Life*

www.ingramcontent.com/pod-product-compliance
Lightning Source LLC
LaVergne TN
LVHW041346080426
835512LV00006B/633